Cool Hotels
Weekend

teNeues

Imprint

Produced by fusion publishing GmbH, Berlin   www.fusion-publishing.com

Edited by Sandra-Mareike Kreß, fusion publishing; Hotel scouting by Patricia Massó, fusion publishing
Editorial coordination by Verena von Holtum, teNeues Verlag; Sandra-Mareike Kreß, fusion publishing
Text by Sandra-Mareike Kreß; Translations by Bochert Translations
Layout, pre-press & imaging by fusion publishing

Cover photo (location): © Brown's Hotel (Brown's Hotel)
Back cover photos from top to bottom (location): © Brown's Hotel (Brown's Hotel), © Casa Fuster (Casa Fuster), Klaus Frahm /
© SIDE Hotel (SIDE Hotel), © Mandarin Oriental, Munich (Mandarin Oriental, Munich), © Cerês (Cerês)

Photos (location): Attila Szabó, Rudolf Klein (Lánchíd 19), Carlo Valentini (Riva Lofts), © Berns Hotel (p. 7 r., Berns Hotel),
© BRANDENBURGER HOF (BRANDENBURGER HOF Berlin), © Brown's Hotel (Brown's Hotel), © Bulgari Hotels & Resorts
(Bulgari Hotels & Resorts Milano), © Casa Fuster (p. 9 r., Casa Fuster), © Cerês (Cerês), © Dylan Hotel Dublin (Dylan),
© First Hotel Skt. Petri (p. 6 r., First Hotel Skt. Petri), © Gerbermühle (Gerbermühle), © Gräflicher Park (Gräflicher Park Hotel &
Spa), © Gramercy Park Hotel (p. 6 l., Gramercy Park Hotel), © Grande Bretagne (Grande Bretagne), © H1898/de Nuñez y
Navarro Hoteles (H1898), © Hospes Hotels & Moments (Palacio del Bailío), © Hotel Imperial Wien (pp. 90, 92, 94-95 Imperial),
© Hotel Josef (Hotel Josef), © Hotel Julien (Hotel Julien), © Hotel Raphaël (Hotel Raphaël-Relais & Châteaux), © Hotel Sacher
(Sacher), © La Réserve Genève (La Réserve Genève Hotel & Spa), © Mandarin Oriental (Mandarin Oriental, Munich), © Pastis
Hotel (Pastis Hotel St Tropez), © Seven Stars Galleria (Seven Stars Galleria), © The Dorchester (p. 8 r., The Dorchester),
© Thompson (Thompson), © Widder (pp. 108-110 Widder), © Viceroy (p. 5 r., Viceroy Santa Monica), © vigilius mountain
resort (vigilius mountain resort), © Villa Marie (p. 8 l., Villa Marie), Fabrice Rambert/© Hotel Keppler (Hotel Keppler),
Gavin Jackson (Blakes London, Ritz Carlton, pp. 189-190), Heinrich Helfenstein (p. 111 Widder), Hospes Hotels & Moments
(p. 5 l., Hospes Maricel, Palacio de los Patos), Koray Erkaya (pp. 188, 191 Sumahan on the Water), Karin Kohlberg / © The
Lowell (The Lowell Hotel), Klaus Frahm / © SIDE Hotel (p. 4, SIDE Hotel), Matthias Nero (p. 7 l., Puro), Michelle Galindo (p. 9
l., Santo Mauro), Nikolas Koenig (p. 213-215, Standard Miami), The Setai, Hotel AC Palacio del Retiro), Reto Guntli/zapaimages
(Riad Enija), Rocco Forte Hotels (Hotel Amigo), Roland Bauer (Hotel de Filosoof, Kruisherenhotel Maastricht, pp. 91, 93 Imperial, PALACE Luzern, Hôtel Cloître Saint Louis, Radisson Blu Le Dokhan's Hotel)

Price orientation: $ = < 200 $, $$ = 201 $ – 350 $, $$$ = 351 $ – 550 $, $$$$ = > 551 $

Published by teNeues Publishing Group

teNeues Verlag GmbH + Co. KG
Am Selder 37
47906 Kempen, Germany
Tel.: 0049-(0)2152-916-0
Fax: 0049-(0)2152-916-111
E-mail: books@teneues.de

teNeues Publishing Company
16 West 22nd Street
New York, NY 10010, USA
Tel.: 001-212-627-9090
Fax: 001-212-627-9511

teNeues Publishing UK Ltd.
21 Marlowe Court, Lymer Avenue
London, SE19 1LP
Great Britain
Tel.: 0044-208-670-7522
Fax: 0044-208-670-7523

teNeues France S.A.R.L.
39, rue de Billets
18250 Henrichemont
France
Tel.: 0033-2-48269348
Fax: 0033-1-70723482

Press department: arehn@teneues.de
Phone: 0049-2152-916-202

www.teneues.com

ISBN: 978-3-8327-9396-8

© 2010 teNeues Verlag GmbH + Co. KG, Kempen

Printed in China

Bibliographic information published by Die Deutsche Nationalbibliothek.
Die Deutsche Nationalbibliothek lists this publication in the Deutsche Nationalbibliografie;
detailed bibliographic data is available in the Internet at http://dnb.d-nb.de.

Contents   Page

Introduction

Turning our backs on everyday life, simply drifting and seeking fresh inspiration in a new environment—there are many good reasons for a weekend getaway. Everyone can personally choose from a repertoire of fascinating cities that are within easy reach and worth visiting for a couple of days.

Vibrant arts scenes, endless shopping facilities and innovative catering offers make cities such as Barcelona, Paris, Vienna, New York and London ideal travel destinations. The hotels in these cities amaze their guests with fancy design, state-of-the-art facilities and individual service. They are situated right in the hub of activity. Because visitors with limited time would not want to sacrifice it for a long journey.

Guests seeking relaxation enjoy remote hideaways more so than the adventure of a pulsating city. With great comfort and exclusive wellness offers hotel guests can be pampered in the Swiss mountains, on the coast of Saint-Tropez or under the California sun—and can return to their everyday life feeling refreshed and rested.

Those not wanting to go without exciting experiences or relaxation on their short break will also find an exciting combination of the two in picking the right hotel. How you experience a city depends on how you live there. The cool hotels that especially enhance the weekend are revealed on the following pages.

Sandra-Mareike Kreß

Einleitung

Dem Alltag den Rücken zukehren, sich treiben lassen und in einer neuen Umgebung nach frischer Inspiration suchen – es gibt viele gute Gründe für einen Wochenendurlaub. Nach persönlichem Geschmack kann jeder aus einem Repertoire faszinierender Metropolen und Landstriche wählen, die schnell erreichbar sind und sich bereits für ein paar Tage lohnen.

Lebendige Kunstszenen, grenzenlose Einkaufsmöglichkeiten und innovative Gastronomie-angebote machen Städte wie Barcelona, Paris, Wien, New York oder London zu idealen Reisezielen. In ihnen finden sich Hotels, die durch ausgefallenes Design, modernste Ausstattung und individuellen Service ihre Gäste ins Staunen versetzen. Sie befinden sich mitten im Zentrum des Geschehens. Denn wer nur wenig Zeit mitbringt, möchte diese nicht für lange Wege opfern.

Rundum Erholungsbedürftige suchen weniger das Abenteuer einer pulsierenden Großstadt, sondern erfreuen sich an abgelegenen Hideaways. Mit umfassendem Komfort und exklusiven Wellness-Angeboten lassen sich Hotelgäste in den Schweizer Bergen, an der Küste von Saint-Tropez oder unter der Sonne Kaliforniens verwöhnen – und können erfrischt und ausgeruht in den Alltag zurückkehren.

Wer in seinem Kurzurlaub weder aufregende Erlebnisse noch Entspannung missen möchte, findet mit Hilfe des passenden Hotels auch eine genussvolle Kombination aus beidem. Denn wie man eine Stadt erlebt, hängt sehr davon ab, wie man dort wohnt. Welche coolen Hotels das Wochenende auf besondere Weise veredeln, verraten die kommenden Seiten.

Sandra-Mareike Kreß

Introduction

Oublier le train-train quotidien, donner libre court à ses envies et se ressourcer dans un nouvel environnement: de bonnes raisons pour s'offrir un week-end de détente. Selon les envies de chacun, le répertoire permet de choisir entre de fascinantes métropoles ou des recoins perdus. Des destinations faciles à atteindre, idéales pour un court séjour.

Une vie artistique bouillonnante, des offres illimitées de shopping et des propositions gastronomiques innovantes convertissent des villes comme Barcelone, Paris, Vienne, New York ou Londres en destinations idéales. Vous y trouverez des hôtels qui vous surprendront par leur design singulier, leur équipement ultramoderne et l'attention personnalisée accordée à leurs clients. Vous vous retrouverez au centre des événements. Si vous n'avez que peu de temps disponible, vous ne souhaitez certainement pas l'investir dans le trajet.

À la recherche de détente et de repos, vous recherchez plutôt les petits recoins tranquilles et perdus, au lieu de vous plonger dans la vie trépidante des grandes villes. Les clients profitent du grand confort et des offres exclusives de bien-être proposés aussi bien par les hôtels des montagnes suisses, de la baie de Saint-Tropez que ceux situés sous le soleil californien. Le retour à la vie quotidienne se fera avec des énergies renouvelées et détendu.

Vous ne voulez renoncer ni à la détente ni à vivre des vacances inoubliables ? En sélectionnant l'établissement adéquat, vous pourrez profiter de cette excellente combinaison. Découvrir une ville dépend en grande mesure du mode de vie de ses habitants. Découvrez dans les pages suivantes les hôtels sympas qui agrémenteront particulièrement votre week-end.

Sandra-Mareike Kreß

Introducción

Escapar de la rutina de la vida diaria, dejarse llevar y buscar nueva inspiración en un entorno diferente –existen un sinfín de razones para tomarse un fin de semana de vacaciones. Dependiendo de lo que más le guste, podrá elegir de entre un amplio repertorio de fascinantes metrópolis y regiones rápidamente accesibles y en las que merece la pena pasar un par de días.

Su animado ambiente artístico, sus ilimitadas posibilidades para ir de compras y su innovadora oferta gastronómica convierten a ciudades como Barcelona, París, Viena, Nueva York o Londres en excelentes destinos turísticos. En ellas encontrará hoteles capaces de sorprender a sus huéspedes por su extraordinario diseño, su moderno equipamiento y su servicio personalizado. Estos hoteles están situados en las mejores ubicaciones de la ciudad. De esta forma, si no dispone de mucho tiempo, no lo perderá en ir de un lado a otro de la ciudad.

Aquellos que buscan sobre todo unos días de relax están menos interesados en las aventuras que brinda una gran ciudad y prefieren disfrutar de parajes más apartados del bullicio. Estos huéspedes pueden dejarse mimar por el máximo confort y nuestras exclusivas ofertas de wellness en las montañas suizas, en la costa de Saint-Tropez o bajo el sol de California, para regresar frescos y renovados a la rutina de la vida diaria.

Si desea tomarse una pequeñas vacaciones y no perderse nada de la ciudad, pero disfrutar también de un tiempo de relax, en esta guía encontrará el hotel adecuado para lograr esa perfecta combinación. Y es que la manera en la que se disfruta de una ciudad depende mucho del lugar en el que se aloje. En las siguientes páginas descubrirá cuáles son los hoteles ideales para disfrutar al máximo de un fin de semana.

Sandra-Mareike Kreß

Introduzione

Evadere dalla vita di tutti i giorni, abbandonarsi al relax e trovare nuovi spunti di ispirazione in un nuovo ambiente – sono molti i buoni motivi per una breve vacanza di un fine settimana. Ognuno può scegliere seguendo il proprio gusto personale; il repertorio prevede metropoli e regioni affascinanti facilmente raggiungibili, che meritano sicuramente una breve visita.

Scenari pieni di vita, infinite possibilità per lo shopping e innovative offerte gastronomiche - questo rende città come Barcellona, Parigi, Vienna, New York o Londra mete di viaggio ideali. Vi si trovano hotel che sorprendono gli ospiti per l'insolito design, l'arredamento ultramoderno ed un servizio individuale. Ci si ritrova nel cuore degli eventi. Poiché chi ha poco tempo a disposizione non può sacrificarlo per percorrere lunghi tragitti.

Chi ha bisogno di relax non cerca l'avventura in una vivace metropoli ma aspira a raggiungere rifugi sperduti. Tra le montagne svizzere, sulla costa di Saint-Tropez o sotto il sole della California gli ospiti possono farsi coccolare da esclusive offerte-benessere in ambienti assolutamente confortevoli – così possono ritornare alla vita quotidiana ritemprati e rilassati.

Anche il turista che nella sua breve vacanza volesse vivere esperienze stimolanti senza però rinunciare al relax può trovare una giusta combinazione scegliendo l'hotel adatto. Poiché per conoscere una città bisogna anche tener conto di come ci si soggiorna. Le pagine che seguono suggeriscono quali sono gli hotel alla moda che riescono a trasformare il fine settimana in un'esperienza molto particolare.

Sandra-Mareike Kreß

Berns Hotel

Näckströmsgatan 8
11147 Stockholm
Sweden
Phone: +46 / 8 / 56 63 22 00
Fax: +46 / 8 / 56 63 22 01
www.berns.se

Price category: $$
Rooms: 82 rooms, 3 suites
Facilities: Gym and spa facilities, complimentary high-speed Internet, 2 restaurants, terrace bars, clubs, China Theater
Services: Concierge service
Located: In the heart of the commercial district
Public transportation: Norrmalstorg
Map: No. 1
Style: Contemporary design
What's special: The nightlife in the Berns, popular among locals as well, is a must for the guests of the hotel: it boasts a large dance floor, three differently themed bars and a small club in the basement.

Blakes Hotel London

33 Roland Gardens
London SW7 3PF
United Kingdom
Phone: +44 / 20 / 73 70 67 01
Fax: +44 / 20 / 73 73 04 42
www.blakeshotels.com

Price category: $$$
Rooms: 50 rooms and suites
Facilities: Restaurant and private meeting room, wedding ceremonies in Suite 007
Services: Room service
Located: In the quiet quarter of South Kensington, near Brompton Cross and Kings Road
Public transportation: South Kensington, Gloucester Road
Map: No. 2
Style: Fashionable mixture of modern and Far Eastern design
What's special: Created by acclaimed British designer Anouska Hempel, the hotel is an architectural statement of uniqueness and originality—all rooms are individually themed.

Brown's Hotel

Albemarle Street
London W1S 4BP
United Kingdom
Phone: +44 / 20 / 74 93 60 20
Fax: +44 / 20 / 75 18 40 64
www.roccofortecollection.com

Price category: $$$$
Rooms: 88 rooms and 29 suites
Facilities: Restaurant, tea room & bar, private dining rooms, 3 spa treatment rooms
Services: Wedding licence, 6 private dining rooms, 24 h inroom dining, 24 h gym, luxurious spa treatments, babysitting, bar with live jazz, Top London Afternoon Tea
Located: Just a few steps from Piccadilly and the elegant shops of Bond Street
Public transportation: Green Park, Piccadilly Circus
Map: No. 3
Style: Sophisticated elegance
What's special: Sophistication and classic English style are the hallmarks of the most historic hotel in London. A long-held British institution: afternoon tea in the hotel's English Tea Room.

The Dorchester

Park Lane
London W1K 1QA
United Kingdom
Phone: +44 / 20 / 76 29 88 88
Fax: +44 / 20 / 76 29 80 80
www.thedorchester.com

Price category: $$$$
Rooms: 250 guestrooms
Facilities: Restaurant, bar, spa, meeting, banquet
Services: In-suite check in, e-butler service, WiFi, florist, roof suites: personalised butler service
Located: At Hyde Park
Public transportation: Hyde Park Corner
Map: No. 4
Style: Classic British elegance
What's special: This five star hotel offers elegant rooms, all providing views over Hyde Park or the hotel's landscaped terraces. Guests enjoy modern french cuisine in Alain Ducasse, which was honoured with two Michelin stars.

Dylan

Eastmoreland Place
Dublin 4
Ireland
Phone: +353 / 1 / 660 30 00
Fax: +353 / 1 / 660 30 05
www.dylan.ie

Price category: $$$
Rooms: 44 rooms including 5 suites
Facilities: Dylanbar, Still Restaurant, The Library, private dining room
Services: Concierge, 24 h room service, valet parking
Located: In the city center, just a 10 min walk from St. Stephens Green
Public transportation: Baggot St. Bridge
Map: No. 5
Style: Boutique hotel
What's special: The mix of ultra-modern designer furniture and carefully mixed in antiques makes up its exceptional atmosphere. The contemporary technological equipment includes plasma TVs, Internet access, iPod stations, as well as floor heating in the puristic styled baths.

First Hotel Skt. Petri

Krystalgade 22
1172 Copenhagen
Denmark
Phone: +45 / 33 / 45 91 00
Fax: +45 / 33 / 45 91 10
www.hotelsktpetri.com

Price category: $$
Rooms: 268 rooms and suites including 1 penthouse
Facilities: Bar, restaurant, café, fitness
Services: Concierge, massage, private yoga, 24 h room service, broadband Internet access
Located: In the old Latin Quarter of Copenhagen
Public transportation: Nørreport
Map: No. 6
Style: Modern Scandinavian
What's special: Copenhagen's hippest hotel bears witness to the quality of Scandinavian design: functionality, timeless modernity and reduction to essentials. Situated in a quiet corner of the old city, a grand view opens out over the roofs of the Nordic metropolis on the upper floors.

Hotel de Filosoof

Anna van den Vondelstraat 6
1054 GZ Amsterdam
Netherlands
Phone: +31 / 20 / 683 30 13
Fax: +31 / 20 / 685 37 50
www.hotelfilosoof.nl

Price category: $
Rooms: 38 rooms
Facilities: Bar, lounge, library, spacious garden, meeting rooms
Services: WiFi access by request, 24 h room service, 100% non-smoking guestrooms
Located: In walking distance to all main museums, art galleries as well as shopping and entertainment areas
Public transportation: Jan Pieter Heijestraat
Map: No. 7
Style: Contemporary design
What's special: Each room in the three 19th-century buildings is individually decorated and devoted to either a famous poet, a thinker or a philosophic script. Readings are hosted frequently.

Moral virtue is a mean between two vices one of excess and the other of deficiency It aims at hitting the meanpoint in feelings and actions

The ethics of Aristotle

Kruisherenhotel Maastricht

Kruisherengang 19–23
6211 NW Maastricht
Netherlands
Phone: +31 / 43 / 329 20 20
Fax: +31 / 43 / 323 30 30
www.chateauhotels.nl

Price category: $$
Rooms: 32 rooms and 28 suites
Facilities: Winebar Rouge & Blanc, Kruisherenrestaurant, lounge corners, library, garden
Services: 24 h room service, limousine service, babysitting, dog walking, bicycles and Vespas available
Located: In the city center
Public transportation: Wolder, Kommelplein
Map: No. 8
Style: Design hotel
What's special: The 15th-century monastery is certain to transfer a traveler into another dimension. Design classics, wall paintings and the lighting magician Ingo Maurer's conception round off the artistic ensemble. Breakfast is served in the gallery with a breathtaking view of Maastricht.

Hotel Amigo

1–3, rue de l'Amigo
1000 Brussels
Belgium
Phone: +32 / 2 / 547 47 47
Fax: +32 / 2 / 513 52 77
www.roccofortecollection.com

Price category: $$$$
Rooms: 173 rooms and 19 suites
Facilities: Bar, restaurant, fitness center
Services: Concierge, children's amenities
Located: Situated in the heart of Brussels, next to the picturesque Grand Place
Public transportation: Bourse Beurs
Map: No. 9
Style: Modern classic
What's special: In the 16th century, the house which today accommodates hotel guests served as a prison. Thanks to renovation works, nothing is left to remind the guests of the previous role of the distinguished luxury hotel whose design is clearly marked by famous designer Olga Polizzi.

Hotel Julien

Korte Nieuwstraat 24
2000 Antwerp
Belgium
Phone: +32 / 3 / 229 06 00
Fax: +32 / 3 / 233 35 70
www.hotel-julien.com

Price category: $$
Rooms: 11 rooms
Facilities: Breakfast room, library, lounge
Services: Free WiFi, laundry and dry cleaning, babysitting, DVD and CD library, 24 h front desk, non-smoking rooms, choice of newspapers and magazines
Located: In the old city center
Public transportation: Melkmarkt
Map: No. 10
Style: Modern classic design
What's special: Two of the typical narrow 16th-century buildings in Antwerp house the wonderful small hotel. Classical modern furniture largely by Ray and Charles Eames are combined with light materials to make up the friendly atmosphere.

Hotel Josef

Rybná 20
11000 Prague 1
Czech Republic
Phone: +420 / 2 / 21 70 01 11
Fax: +420 / 2 / 21 70 09 99
www.hoteljosef.com

Price category: $
Rooms: 109 rooms in 2 houses
Facilities: Garden, conference room, business center, garage, gym, sauna, massage room
Services: Concierge service and guest relations
Located: In the center of Prague, 5 min from the Old Town Square, near the Jewish quarter
Public transportation: Dlouhá třída
Map: No. 11
Style: Modern design
What's special: The trendy colors orange and pink dominate the modern interior design. None of the rooms looks alike. And often enough guests will find a bathtub in the middle of the room, only separated by a see-through glass wall. A vegetated courtyard and a roof terrace belong to the many assets of this hotel.

Lánchíd 19

Lánchíd utca 19
1013 Budapest
Hungary
Phone: +36 / 1 / 419 19 00
Fax: +36 / 1 / 419 19 19
www.lanchid19hotel.hu

Price category: $
Rooms: 48 rooms including 3 suites
Facilities: Restaurant, bar, 3 meeting rooms
Services: Laundry, cultural program organization, change, business services
Located: In the city center, by the Danube
Public transportation: Clark Ádám tér
Map: No. 12
Style: Modern
What's special: In a street characterized by 19th-century buildings, this hotel designed in contemporary style stands out like a sparkling jewel. Its glass facades are illuminated in the dark by large-format pictures. The rooms and suites are furnished in minimalist style that perfectly brings out the effect of their designer furniture.

Fax: +49 / 38393 / 66 67 68
www.ceres-hotel.de

Located: Directly at the Baltic Sea
Public transportation: Binz station
Map: No. 13
Style: Contemporary design
What's special: This hotel offers its guests a balcony
or terrace in each room. The Senso Spa is the intimate
setting for a journey towards inner balance, it offers exclu-
sive treatments and is driven solely by the power of water.

BRANDENBURGER HOF Berlin

Eislebener Straße 14
10789 Berlin
Germany
Phone: +49 / 30 / 21 40 50
Fax: +49 / 30 / 21 40 51 00
www.brandenburger-hof.com

Price category: $$$
Rooms: 58 rooms, 14 suites
Facilities: Restaurant, bar, lounge, library, business center, sauna, indoor pool, garden, private parking
Services: Room service, airport shuttle, babysitting service, laundry, dry cleaning, bridal suite, bicycle rental, tour desk, ticket service, free access to the nearby sports club
Located: In the Center of Berlin, close to Kurfürstendamm and Gedächtniskirche
Public transportation: Zoologischer Garten
Map: No. 14
Style: Sophisticated elegance
What's special: Close to the famous Kurfürstendamm shopping district, the Gedächtniskirche memorial church, and excellent public transport links, this five star hotel offers its guests understated luxury and elegance.

Ritz Carlton

Potsdamer Platz 3
10785 Berlin
Germany
Phone: +49 / 30 / 33 77 77
Fax: +49 / 30 / 337 77 55 55
www.ritzcarlton.com

Price category: $$$
Rooms: 303 rooms including 40 suites
Facilities: French brasserie, tea lounge, club bar, business center, spa, jacuzzi, saunas, indoor pool, gym
Services: Touch-screen room controls, in-room Internet, in-room laptop safe, laundry and dry cleaning services
Located: In the center of Berlin at Potsdamer Platz
Public transportation: Potsdamer Platz
Map: No. 15
Style: Luxury
What's special: Here guests can enjoy La Prairie Boutique Spa treatments and go for a swim in the elegant pool under the sparkling crystal ceiling. Each of the guestrooms and suites are distinguished by original watercolors being created by Professor Markus Luepertz, a German artist highly noted for his 20th century neo-expressionism style.

Gräflicher Park Hotel & Spa

Brunnenallee 1
33014 Bad Driburg
Germany
Phone: +49 / 5253 / 952 30
Fax: +49 / 5253 / 952 32 05
www.graeflicher-park.de

Price category: $$
Rooms: 135 rooms and suites
Facilities: 2 restaurants, fusion bar, spa area based on own mineral spring, gym, heated outdoor pool, exclusive private spa suites, 18-holes golf course
Services: Babysitter service, WiFi, arrangement of transportation
Located: 35 km from Paderborn airport, 150 km from Hannover airport, ICE train station Altenbeken
Public transportation: Bad Driburg (Westf)
Map: No. 16
Style: Country house design with modern elements
What's special: Situated in a large park at the gates of Teutoburg Forest, the complex features a 5-square-kilometers spa. Lawn-tennis, golf and opportunities for hunting complete the services.

SIDE Hotel

Drehbahn 49
20354 Hamburg
Germany
Phone: +49 / 40 / 30 99 90
Fax: +49 / 40 / 30 99 93 99
www.side-hamburg.de

Price category: $$
Rooms: 178 rooms including 10 suites
Facilities: High end steakhouse [m]eatery, cocktailbar, upper floor terrace with 360-degree views of the skyline
Services: Spa treatments, room service, babysitting, concierge, cookery course
Located: Located right in the city center
Public transportation: Gänsemarkt
Map: No. 17
Style: Urban minimalist elegance
What's special: The SIDE hotel was designed by architect Jan Störmer while the puristic interior design carries the fingerprint of Italian designer Matteo Thun. All rooms are dominated by warm and light colors. From the Sky Lounge on the eighth floor guests can enjoy the marvelous view over the rooftops of Hamburg.

Gerbermühle

Gerbermühlstraße 105
60594 Frankfurt
Germany
Phone: +49 / 69 / 68 97 77 90
Fax: +49 / 69 / 689 77 79 66
www.gerbermuehle.com

Price category: $$
Rooms: 7 single rooms, 6 double rooms, 5 suites
Facilities: Restaurant, winter garden with terrace, summer garden, bar
Services: Babysitting, personal trainer on request, 24 h room service, free WiFi
Located: On the bank of the river Main, close to historical Frankfurt-Sachsenhausen and the city center
Public transportation: Offenbach Kaiserlei
Map: No. 18
Style: Modern design with traditional details
What's special: Guests relax in the futuristic glass-walled dining area, the minimalist lodge-style café or the 500-seat summer garden covered by ornate white umbrellas.

Mandarin Oriental, Munich

Neuturmstraße 1
80331 Munich
Germany
Phone: +49 / 89 / 29 09 80
Fax: +49 / 89 / 22 25 39
www.mandarinoriental.com

Price category: $$$
Rooms: 73 rooms including 25 suites and junior suites
Facilities: Restaurant Mark's (Michelin star), Mandarin Bar, outdoor swimming pool on the roof terrace, BistroMO, Cigar and Rum Club
Services: High level of personalised service
Located: In the historic city center
Public transportations: Marienplatz, Isartor
Map: No. 19
Style: Modern classic
What's special: The credo of the architect was to preserve the historical character of the neo-Renaissance ballroom building. Thus, French and Italian marble, cherry and ebony wood dominate the appearance of the hotel. The guests enjoy the exquisite dishes of one of the Munich's five leading gourmet restaurants based here.

Imperial

Kärntner Ring 16
1015 Vienna
Austria
Phone: +43 / 1 / 50 11 00
Fax: +43 / 1 / 50 11 04 10
www.luxurycollection.com/imperial

Price category: $$$$
Rooms: 138 rooms, 32 suites
Facilities: Bar Maria Theresia, Restaurant Imperial, Café Imperial, fitness and health studio, 7 meeting rooms
Services: Concierge and butler service, Internet access, limousine service
Located: Close to major sites and shopping area
Public transportation: Schwarzenbergplatz, Wien Oper
Map: No. 20
Style: Timeless elegance of 19th-century Vienna
What's special: The noble hotel opened in 1873. Valuable antiques and an opulent collection of paintings and chandelliers endow the hotel with aristocratic atmosphere. The Imerial Butler takes pride in delighting discerning travelers, those who are accustomed to staying at the best addresses.

Sacher

Philharmonikerstraße 4
1010 Vienna
Austria
Phone: +43 / 1 / 51 45 60
Fax: +43 / 1 / 51 45 68 10
www.sacher.com

Price category: $$$$
Rooms: 152 rooms including suites
Facilities: 2 restaurants, café, confiserie, traditional banquet halls, spa, conference facilities
Services: Concierge, limousine service, WiFi
Located: In the heart of the city, opposite the Opera House
Public transportation: Albertinaplatz, Walfischgasse/ Kärntner Strasse
Map: No. 21
Style: Classic elegance with antique details
What's special: The renovation did not harm the Habsburg charm of this five star hotel. The restaurants serve light international cuisine and traditional Viennese dishes, and the Original Sacher-Torte is available in the famous Café Sacher.

La Réserve Genève Hotel & Spa

301, route de Lausanne
1293 Geneva
Switzerland
Phone: +41 / 22 / 959 59 59
Fax: +41 / 22 / 959 59 60
www.lareserve.ch

Price category: $$$$
Rooms: 102 rooms and suites
Facilities: Spa with 17 treatment rooms, art gym, indoor and outdoor pool, sauna, hammam
Services: Private jet, boat with captain, boutique, open-air playground for kids, babysitting, beauty treatments
Located: On the right shore of Lake Geneva. 5 km from the center of Geneva, 3 km from the International Airport
Public transportation: Les Tuileries
Map: No. 22
Style: Cozy elegance
What's special: Star designer Jacques Garcia takes guests in the hotel's unusual rooms on a "static journey." The lobby-lounge was designed in the style of an African safari lodge. In contrast, the 2,000-square-meters spa is kept entirely in cream-white.

PALACE Luzern

Haldenstraße 10
6002 Lucerne
Switzerland
Phone: +41 / 41 / 416 16 16
Fax: +41 / 41 / 416 10 00
www.palace-luzern.ch

Price category: $$$$
Rooms: 136 light and airy rooms and suites
Facilities: Restaurants, bar, spa, 13 event rooms
Services: WiFi, concierge, in-house business center
Located: In the heart of Switzerland at Lake Lucerne, about 1 h from Zurich and Basel airports
Public transportation: Schweizerhofquai, Gärtnerstrasse
Map: No. 23
Style: Modern classic
What's special: The belle époque-style building is situated directly by the Lake Lucerne. From most of the rooms guests have a gorgeous view of the lake, the mountains or the historic city center. The Palace spa offers a range of personalized programmes combining traditional oriental treatments with selected western techniques.

Widder

Rennweg 7
8001 Zurich
Switzerland
Phone: +41 / 44 / 224 25 26
Fax: +41 / 44 / 224 24 24
www.widderhotel.ch

Price category: $$$
Rooms: 42 rooms and 7 suites
Facilities: Restaurant and bar, small technogym, library, business center, 8 conference rooms
Services: 24 h room service, concierge, valet service, WiFi, interactive B&O screen TV and stereo
Located: In the heart of Zurich's historic city center
Public transportation: Rennweg, Storchen
Map: No. 24
Style: Sophisticated, classic design
What's special: The hotel consists of nine historic townhouses that are connected by different stairways and courtyards. In the guest and common rooms, impressive furniture and art objects of Le Corbusier, Mies van der Rohe and Ray Eames can be found.

Hôtel Cloître Saint Louis

20, rue du Portail Boquier
84000 Avignon
France
Phone: +33 / 4 / 90 27 55 55
Fax: +33 / 4 / 90 82 24 01
www.cloitre-saint-louis.com

Price category: $$
Rooms: 80 rooms
Facilities: Restaurant, rooftop terrace, outdoor pool, garden, parking
Services: Room service, satellite TV, free WiFi in lobby
Located: In the heart of Avignon
Public transportation: Bus, TGV train station
Map: No. 25
Style: Modern
What's special: Anyone wanting to live in the papal city of Avignon in true style is at the best address here: the Hôtel Cloître Saint Louis was built in the 16th century as a Jesuit monastery—today it combines the old architecture effectively with a modern addition designed by Jean Nouvel. Especially in summer, guests enjoy the roof pool and the idyllic inner courtyard with its mighty plane trees.

10, rue Kepler
75016 Paris
France
Phone: +33 / 1 / 47 20 65 05
Fax: +33 / 1 / 47 23 02 29
www.keppler-paris-hotel.com

Price category: $$$
Rooms: 39 rooms including 4 suites and 1 penthouse
Facilities: Bar, fitness room including steam room, sauna and gym
Services: Clé d'Or concierge service, WiFi, room service, laundry, facilities for the disabled, parking
Located: In a quiet street next to the Champs-Elysées
Public transportation: Georges V and Charles de Gaulle – Etoile
Map: No. 26
Style: Modern
What's special: The designer Pierre Yves Rochon has created a perfect example of the famous French elegance. The ambience of the hotel is intimate and homelike. The top floor suites have superb terraces or balconies overlooking Paris and the Eiffel Tower.

Radisson Blu Le Dokhan's Hotel

117, rue Lauriston
75116 Paris
France
Phone: +33 / 1 / 53 65 66 99
Fax: +33 / 1 / 53 65 66 88
www.radissonblu.com

Price category: $$$
Rooms: 41 rooms and 4 suites
Facilities: Champagne-Bar
Services: Free high-speed Internet, express & late check-out
Located: Between the Trocadéro and Arc de Triomphe
Public transportations: Trocadéro and Victor Hugo
Map: No. 27
Style: Neoclassic
What's special: Interior designer Frédéric Méchiche made a stylish boutique hotel with plenty of atmosphere out of the city palace in the noble 16th arrondissement of Paris. The intimate bar offers modern French cuisine besides the finest brands of champagne. An elevator is a real extra—made out of a wardrobe trunk by Louis Vuitton.

Pastis Hotel St Tropez

61, avenue du Général Leclerc
83990 Saint-Tropez
France
Phone: +33 / 4 / 98 12 56 50
Fax: +33 / 4 / 94 96 99 82
www.pastis-st-tropez.com

Price category: $$$
Rooms: 9 rooms
Facilities: Bar, heated pool, boules terrain, meeting room, private parking
Services: WiFi, DVD players in rooms, daily newspapers
Located: A 5 min walk from the heart of the village and the port of Saint-Tropez
Map: No. 28
Style: Contemporary-Provençal
What's special: The hotel was once a Provençal house, now re-created and run by a couple from London, with their own upbeat, personal and eclectic style. There is no stuffy dress code here—although you can run into the young high society.

Villa Marie

Route des Plages
Chemin Val de Rian
83350 Ramatuelle
France
Phone: +33 / 494 / 97 40 22
Fax: +33 / 494 / 97 37 55
www.sibuethotels-spa.com

Price category: $$$
Rooms: 42 bedrooms
Facilities: Restaurant with terrace, bar, shop, spa, outdoor fitness room
Services: Concierge, porter, room service, WiFi, car parking
Located: In Ramatuelle, 10 min drive from Saint-Tropez and from Pampelonne Bay's famous beaches
Map: No. 29
Style: Mediterranean
What's special: Hidden in the heart of a parasol pine wood, Villa Marie overlooks the Bay of Pampelonne and offers a magnificent view of the sea.

Palacio del Bailío

Ramírez de las Casas
de Deza, 10–12
14001 Córdoba
Spain
Phone: +34 / 95 / 749 89 93
Fax: +34 / 95 / 749 89 94
www.hospes.com

Price category: $$
Rooms: 50 rooms, 2 suites and 1 big loft suite
Facilities: Restaurant, tapas bar, lounge bar, spa with pool and roman baths, meeting rooms
Services: Spa utilizes ancient treatments and massage
Located: In the city center
Map: No. 30
Style: Modern elegance in ancient surrounding
What's special: Once a grand working palace, this 17th-century building is now host to a charming oasis of luxury and peace in the heart of Córdoba. Moorish archways, impressive frescos and precious paintings were carefully restored and complemented by elegant furniture in natural colors. A successful symbiosis of the past and the present.

Casa Fuster

Passeo de Gracia, 132
08008 Barcelona
Spain
Phone: +34 / 93 / 255 30 00
Fax: +34 / 93 / 255 30 02
www.hotelcasafuster.com

Price category: $$$
Rooms: 75 rooms, 21 suites
Facilities: 2 restaurants, Café Vienés, rooftop pool, jacuzzi, 10 meeting rooms
Services: Free WiFi, first class service
Located: Just steps away from Passeo de Gracia
Public transportation: Diagonal
Map: No. 31
Style: Combination of contemporary and traditional design
What's special: This luxury hotel has long been on the list of top hotels in Spain. The property is situated on the highest point of the modernistic residential and business district Eixample. From the roof terrace, guests are offered a fantastic view across the city all the way to the ocean.

H1898

La Rambla, 109
(Entrance via C/Pintor Fortuny)
08002 Barcelona
Spain
Phone: +34 / 93 / 552 95 52
Fax: +34 / 93 / 552 95 50
www.hotel1898.com

Price category: $$
Rooms: 169 rooms and 3 suites with terrace and pool
Facilities: Spa, gym, outdoor swimming pool, solarium, meeting rooms, business center, library
Services: Specialised staff for treatments and therapies, free WiFi, parking, turndown service
Located: In the heart of Barcelona at La Rambla
Public transportation: Liceu, Catalunya
Map: No. 32
Style: Colonial and contemporary influences
What's special: The H1898 is an immediate eye-catcher: the facade of the former 19th-century trading house was restored with attention to detail. Some rooms have a private swimming pool or a garden. Public swimming pools for all guests are located in the vaulted cellar and on the roof–with a perfect view of Barcelona.

Palacio de los Patos

Solarillo de Gracia, 1
18002 Granada
Spain
Phone: +34 / 958 / 53 57 90
Fax: +34 / 958 / 53 69 68
www.hospes.com

Price category: $$
Rooms: 42 rooms including 5 suites
Facilities: Restaurant, spa, pool, jacuzzi, sauna and Turkish bath, Arabian garden, meeting rooms
Services: Free Internet, massage & beauty treatments
Located: In the historic center of Granada
Map: No. 33
Style: Combination of antique and modern design
What's special: This former palace is now one of Granada's most intriguing boutique hotels. The spectacular 19th-century building has been transformed into a grand palace for the 21st century by combining it with a new design building with an impressive alabaster facade. The Arabian garden is a great place to find a quiet moment.

Hospes Maricel

Calle d'Andratx, 1
07184 Calvià, Mallorca
Spain
Phone: +34 / 971 / 70 77 44
Fax: +34 / 971 / 70 77 45
www.hospes.com

Price category: $$$
Rooms: 51 rooms and 2 buildings
Facilities: Restaurant, cocktail bar, pool, meeting rooms
Services: Massage therapies
Located: On the beach side, close to Palma de Mallorca, 20 km from Palma airport
Map: No. 34
Style: Contemporary design in ancient surroundings
What's special: This property seems to hover between the sea and the sky, therefore it is named Maricel. Seamless transitions—this pretty much sums up the style of this five star hotel. Contemporary influences were carefully integrated into the stately architecture of the past-century appeal. Raw materials, clear forms and colors are the main aspects of the rooms' decoration.

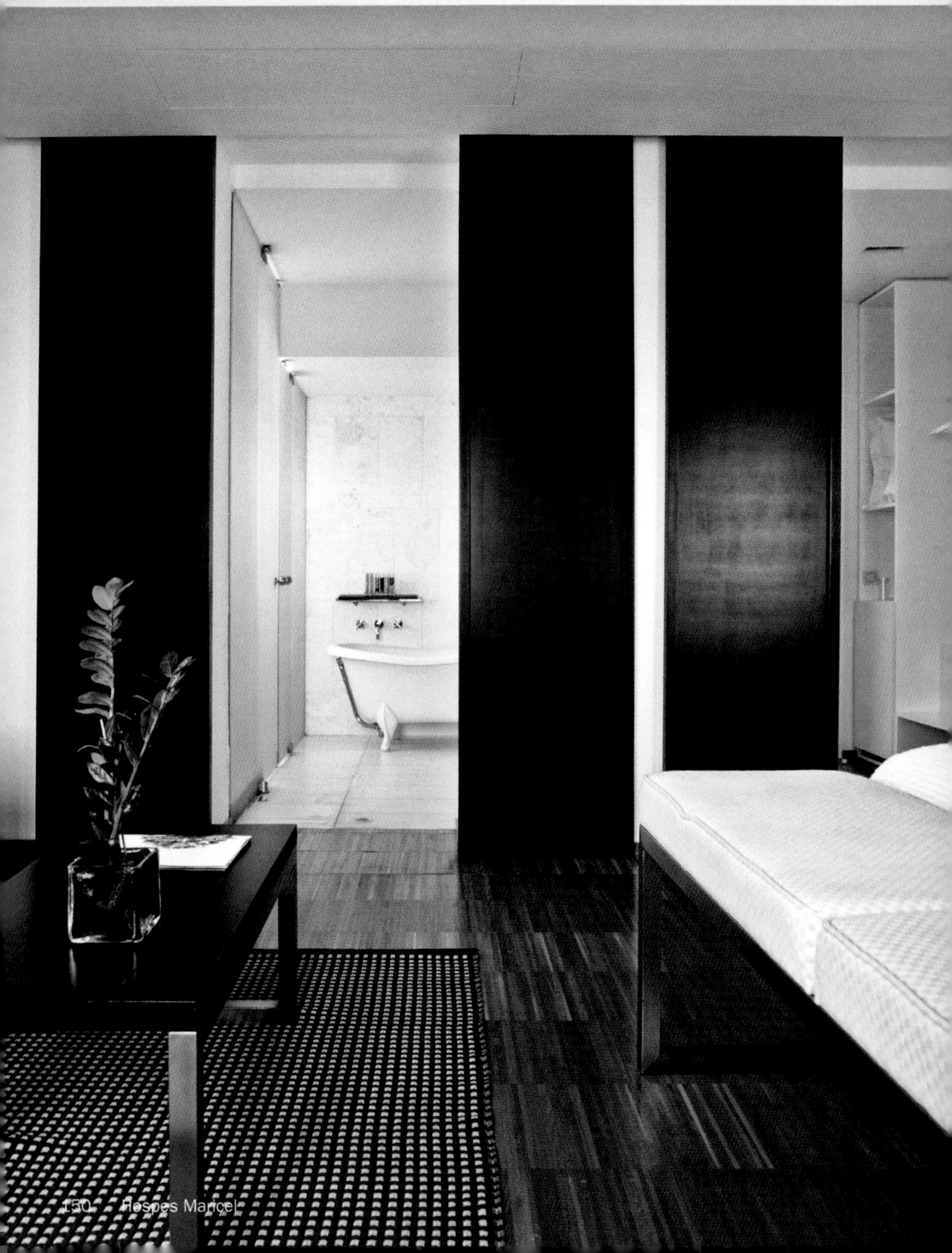

Puro

Montenegro, 12
07012 Palma de Mallorca, Mallorca
Spain
Phone: +34 / 971 / 42 54 50
Fax: +34 / 971 / 42 54 51
www.purohotel.com

Price category: $$
Rooms: 26 rooms and suites
Facilities: Patios, rooftop terrace, restaurant, pool
Services: Concierge, babysitting, massages
Located: Located in Palma's old town La Lonja, next to the historic and shopping districts of Palma
Map: No. 35
Style: Modern ethnic design
What's special: The Puro is known for its appealing interior design and distinctive ambience as well as for its restaurant with its fusion of Mediterranean and Asian cuisine. Within only a short time, it has become one of Palma's hot spots, just like the bar in the hotel's ground floor, where the Palma party crowd can have fun until dawn.

Santo Mauro

Calle Zurbano, 36
28010 Madrid
Spain
Phone: +34 / 91 / 319 69 00
Fax: +34 / 91 / 308 54 77
www.hotelacsantomauro.com

Price category: $$$
Rooms: 51 rooms and suites
Facilities: Restaurant, lobby bar, indoor swimming pool, garden, fitness center
Services: Butler service
Located: In the center of Madrid, close to Paseo de la Castellana
Public transportation: Ruben Darío, Alonso Martinez
Map: No. 36
Style: Classical French style with contemporary elements
What's special: Once the palace of the Marquis of Santo Mauro, nowadays an elegant hotel. In the impressive rooms of the once palace library, the restaurant Santo Mauro offers local specialties and a broad selection of top-class international wines.

Hotel AC Palacio del Retiro

Alfonso XII, 14
28014 Madrid
Spain
Phone: +34 / 91 / 523 74 60
Fax: +34 / 91 / 523 74 61
www.ac-hotels.com

Price category: $$$
Rooms: 50 rooms
Facilities: Restaurant, fitness center, spa, sauna, business facilities, 5 meeting rooms
Services: High-speed Internet, 24 h room service, massage
Located: At the Retiro Park, within the "golden triangle" of the Thyssen, Prado and Reina Sofia museums
Public transportation: Banco de España, Retiro
Map: No. 37
Style: Modern design in ancient surroundings
What's special: The interior is characterized by stucco works, frescos and contemporary stylistic elements. All rooms are individually decorated, and have a modern touch. The restaurant serves creative Mediterranean cuisine.

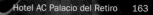

Riva Lofts

Via Baccio Bandinelli 98
50142 Florence
Italy
Phone: +39 / 055 / 713 02 72
Fax: +39 / 055 / 71 11 03
www.rivalofts.com

Price category: $$
Rooms: 9 studios with independent entrance
Facilities: Bar, outdoor pool, 24/7 living room
Services: Concierge, babysitting and massages on request, bikes available for guests
Located: Along the Arno, opposite of Parco delle Cascine
Public transportation: Sansovino
Map: No. 38
Style: Contemporary design
What's special: The Architect Claudio Nardi and his daughter Alice had been rebuilding an old factory near the old town of Florence for years. The result of this effort is Riva Lofts—a residence with nine studios in different sizes, all with puristic design and an elegant arrangement.

Bulgari Hotels & Resorts Milano

Via Privata Fratelli Gabba 7b
20121 Milan, Brera
Italy
Phone: +39 / 02 / 805 80 51
Fax: +39 / 02 / 805 80 52 22
www.bulgarihotels.com

Price category: $$$$
Rooms: 58 rooms and suites
Facilities: Restaurant, bar, lounge, indoor pool, spa, hammam, fitness center, garden, wellness area
Services: Personal shopper, hair & make up service, valet parking, complimentary packing and unpacking service
Located: Located in the heart of Milan, next to the botanical garden
Public transportation: Monte Napoleone
Map: No. 39
Style: Contemporary design
What's special: As one might expect from the famous brand, the hotel is the embodiment of the cool passion that typifies Italian design. The surrounding gardens are a favorite place for Milanese to go chill out.

Seven Stars Galleria

Via Silvio Pellico 8
20121 Milan
Italy
Phone: +39 / 02 / 89 05 82 97
Fax: +39 / 02 / 89 05 82 99
www.townhousegalleria.it

Price category: $$$$
Rooms: 7 suites
Facilities: Restaurant La Sinfonia (only for guests), bar
Services: Events, shopping and art planning, butler assigned to every room
Located: In the heart of Milan
Public transportation: Grossi S.Margherita, Duomo
Map: No. 40
Style: Contemporary elegance in ancient surroundings
What's special: Because the hotel is being approved as the first seven star hotel in the world, the service is flawless. Every suite is attended by its own butler, a personal driver for shopping sprees in Milan is also available. Guests admire the sumptuously adorned windows and hand-painted arched slab, which were carefully restored.

Hotel Raphaël-Relais & Châteaux

Largo Febo 2, Piazza Navona
00186 Rome
Italy
Phone: +39 / 06 / 68 28 31
Fax: +39 / 06 / 687 89 93
www.raphaelhotel.com

Price category: $$$
Rooms: 54 rooms, suites and apartments
Facilities: Restaurant, roof garden, fitness center, meeting facilities, Sala Pantheon, library
Services: Tecnogym, booking service, library, concierge
Located: Centrally located, 20 m from Piazza Navona
Map: No. 41
Style: Modern Italian elegance
What's special: The hotel boasts an almost museum-like arrangement: among other objects of art, a precious collection of Picasso ceramics belongs to the very own treasures of the hotel. Some of the rooms were designed by the star architect Richard Meier. The roof terrace offers an impressive vista of the roofs and domes of the eternal city.

vigilius mountain resort

Vigiljoch
39011 Lana
Italy
Phone: +39 / 0473 / 55 66 00
Fax: +39 / 0473 / 55 66 99
www.vigilius.it

Price category: $$$
Rooms: 35 rooms and 6 suites
Facilities: 2 restaurants, library, yoga room, boccia court
Services: Free activity program, five Tibetan, archery, shiatsu & watsu, wine tasting, yoga
Located: 1,500 m above sea level, reached only by cable car, 8 km to Meran
Public transportation: Cable car
Map: No. 42
Style: Ecological contemporary design
What's special: The grounds feature quartzite-lined indoor pools and outdoor sundecks. Archery and yoga is available for fitness enthusiasts. Cineastes enjoy the film screenings each night in the library.

Grande Bretagne

Constitution Square
10564 Athens
Greece
Phone: +30 / 210 / 333 00 00
Fax: +30 / 210 / 322 80 34
www.grandebretagne.gr

Price category: $$$$
Rooms: 265 rooms, 56 suites
Facilities: Rooftop restaurant, brasserie, café-style restaurant, bar, spa, banquet and meeting facilities, ballroom, wine cellar
Services: Butler service, children's amenities, hair salon, Internet, fitness studio, private transfers
Located: In the center of Athens
Public transportation: Syntagma
Map: No. 43
Style: Modern classic greek design
What's special: Since its opening in 1874, the dignified hotel in the middle of Athens has accommodated just about all the kings, presidents and rulers that the previous century had to offer. Due to a thorough renovation, a modern spa and wellness awaits the guests.

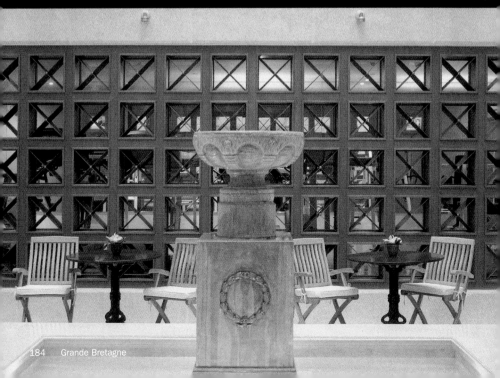

Sumahan on the Water

Kuleli Cadesi 51 Cengelkoy
34684 Istanbul
Turkey
Phone: +90 / 216 / 422 80 00
Fax: +90 / 216 / 422 80 08
www.sumahan.com

Price category: $$
Rooms: 20 rooms and suites with private gardens, almost all have an open fireplace
Facilities: 2 restaurants, wellness center, meeting room
Services: 24 h room service, babysitting, library, accessible for the disabled, fitness and massage service
Located: On the Asian shore of the Bosporus
Public transportation: Kuleli Cad.
Map: No. 44
Style: Sophisticated, classic design
What's special: Located directly by the strait between Europe and Asia, the Sumahan on the Water is an elegant hotel literally built on the water. Guests have a view of the Bosporus from all of the rooms and the terrace café. The restaurant is famous for its fish specialties.

Riad Enija

9 Derb Mesfioui
Rahba Lakdima, Marrakech
Morocco
Phone: +212 / 524 / 44 09 26
Fax: +212 / 524 / 44 27 00
www.riadenija.com

Price category: $$$
Rooms: 7 rooms and 5 suites with private verandas
Facilities: Restaurant offering Moroccan, Eastern and international cuisine
Services: WiFi, airport transfer, excursions, yoga, massage, beauty treatments
Located: Situated in the Medina about 5 min walk from the Jemâa el-Fna square
Public transportation: Gare Routière de Marrakech
Map: No. 45
Style: Oriental elegance
What's special: The property is one of Marrakech's most beautiful privately owned hotels. It has been restored with a love of detail—the mosaics, murals and wood carvings gleam in their old glory. At night the garden and patios are illuminated by candlelight.

Gramercy Park Hotel

2 Lexington Avenue
New York City, NY 10010
USA
Phone: +1 / 212 / 920 33 00
Fax: +1 / 212 / 673 58 90
www.gramercyparkhotel.com

Price category: $$$$
Rooms: 185 guest rooms and luxury suites
Facilities: Restaurant, bars, private roof club, aerospace gym, aerospa, meeting and event rooms, business center
Services: Private key to Gramercy Park, 24 h room service, in-room massage and spa services upon request, concierge, childcare service available upon request
Located: In the heart of Manhattan, directly across from Gramercy Park
Public transportation: 23rd St Station
Map: No. 46
Style: Fashionable luxury
What's special: This famous hotel impresses its guests with extraordinary design, charming atmosphere and first class service.

The Lowell Hotel

28 East 63rd Street
New York City, NY 10065
USA
Phone: +1/ 212 / 838 14 00
Fax: +1 / 212 / 319 42 30
www.lowellhotel.com

Price category: $$$$
Rooms: 49 suites, 23 deluxe rooms
Facilities: 2 restaurants, fitness, private terraces, fireplaces
Services: Concierge, WiFi, business center
Located: Between Madison Avenue and Park Avenue
Public transportation: 59th Street,
Lexington Avenue / 63rd Street
Map: No. 47
Style: A luxurious home from home
What's special: Located on a quiet, tree-lined residential street, the Lowell epitomizes "old New York" luxury. All deluxe rooms and suites are individually decorated with plush carpets, fine antiques, and such ornamental accents as Chinese porcelain bowls, bronze figurines and botanical prints.

Thompson

60 Thompson Street
New York City, NY 10012
USA
Phone: +1 / 877 / 431 04 00
Fax: +1 / 212 / 431 02 00
www.60thompson.com

Price category: $$$$
Rooms: 100 rooms including suites and duplex penthouse
Facilities: Restaurant, rooftop lounge, street café, fitness center
Services: 24 h concierge
Located: In the center of SoHo
Public transportation: Spring St Station
Map: No. 48
Style: Sophisticated elegance
What's special: This established downtown hotel provides guests a luxury environment for an unforgettable new york stay. In the heart of Manhattan's SoHo district, gourmets enjoy authentic Thai cuisine in the hotel's restaurant Kittichai.

Viceroy Santa Monica

1819 Ocean Avenue
Santa Monica, CA 90401
USA
Phone: +1 / 310 / 260 75 00
Fax: +1 / 310 / 260 75 15
www.viceroysantamonica.com

Price category: $$$
Rooms: 162 guestrooms and suites
Facilities: Restaurant, bar, cabanas, two outdoor pools, fitness center, library
Services: WiFi, flat screen TV, 24 h room service
Located: Ocean Avenue and Pico Boulevard
Public transportation: Ocean / Pico
Map: No. 49
Style: English colonial with cosmopolitan spirit
What's special: This modern 8-story seaside refuge combines stylish sophistication with contemporary chic. Guests enjoy the impressive outdoor courtyard dining area with its private cabanas. Most of the rooms have mirrored walls and spectacular ocean views.

Standard Miami

40 Island Avenue
Miami Beach, FL 33139
USA
Phone: +1 / 305 / 673 17 17
www.standardhotels.com

Price category: $$
Rooms: 105 guestrooms with private verandas
Facilities: Restaurant, bayside grill, boutique, gym, luxurious indoor and outdoor spa, Natural Beauty Skincare Clinic, Mud Lounge, yoga center
Services: Free Internet, 24 h room service
Located: On Waters of Belle Isle, 5 min from the beach
Public transportation: Venetian WY at W Island Av
Map: No. 50
Style: Modern creative
What's special: Andre Balazs' fashionable hotel welcomes its guests with colorful design, exclusive cuisine and extraordinary wellness facilities. The spa is concentrating on all forms of water treatments, including a Turkish style hammam, a Swedish sauna and a pool with underwater music installation.

The Setai

2001 Collins Avenue
Miami Beach, FL 33139
USA
Phone: +1 / 305 / 520 60 00
US Toll Free: 888 625 75 00
Fax: +1 / 305 / 520 66 00
www.setai.com

Price category: $$$$
Rooms: 125 suites, penthouse with rooftop pool
Facilities: Spa, 3 pools, hot tub, fitness center, Asian influenced boutique, poolside & beach bar, restaurant, grill
Services: 24 h concierge, babysitting, Internet, yoga, thai chi, watersports, golf, tennis
Located: On the beach of South Beach
Public transportation: Collins Av at 20th St
Map: No. 51
Style: Contemporary and Asian design
What's special: This meticulously replicated Art Deco landmark from the 1930s is now the hippest hotel to hit Miami's glitziest neighborhood. Set amid tropical gardens and sparkling pools this hotel introduces Asian traditions of simplicity and elegance to South Beach.

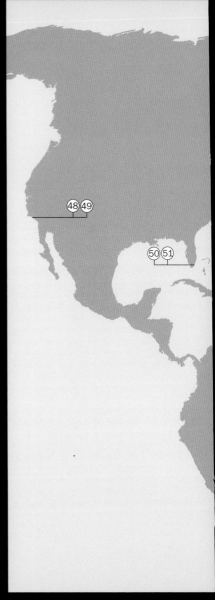

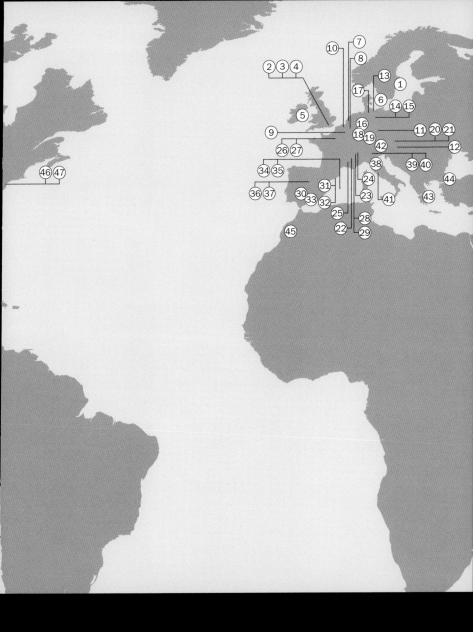

Other titles by teNeues

ISBN 978-3-8327-9309-8

ISBN 978-3-8327-9398-2

ISBN 978-3-8327-9274-9

ISBN 978-3-8327-9237-4

ISBN 978-3-8327-9247-3

ISBN 978-3-8327-9234-3

ISBN 978-3-8327-9308-1

ISBN 978-3-8327-9243-5

ISBN 978-3-8327-9230-5

Size: **15 x 19 cm**, 6 x 7½ in., 224 pp., **Flexicover**, c. 200 color photographs,
Text: English / German / French / Spanish / Italian
www.teneues.com

Other titles by teNeues

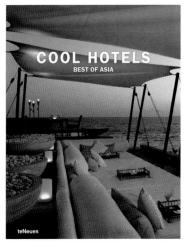

ISBN 978-3-8327-9238-1

ISBN 978-3-8327-9235-0

Size: **25.6 x 32.6 cm**, 10 x 12⁷/₈ in., 396 pp., **Hardcover with jacket**, c. 650 color photographs,
Text: English / German / French / Spanish / Italian
www.teneues.com

teNeues' new Cool Guide series

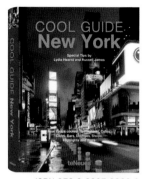

ISBN 978-3-8327-9293-0

ISBN 978-3-8327-9294-7

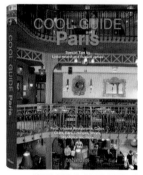

ISBN 978-3-8327-9295-4

ISBN 978-3-8327-9296-1

ISBN 978-3-8327-9236-7

ISBN 978-3-8327-9202-2

Size: **15 x 19 cm**, 6 x 7 ½ in., 224 pp., **Flexicover**, c. 250 color photographs,
Text: English / German / French / Spanish

www.teneues.com